George Ancona Come

and Eat!

ini Charlesbridge

To great-grandkids Maya,
Alexander, and Leila
Love, Poppi George

Published by Charlesbridge
85 Main Street
Watertown, MA 02472
(617) 926-0329
www.charlesbridge.com

Library of Congress Cataloging-in-Publication Data
Ancona, George.
    Come and eat! / George Ancona.
       p. cm.
    ISBN 978-1-58089-366-4 (reinforced for library use)
    ISBN 978-1-58089-367-1 (softcover)
1. Food habits—Juvenile literature. I. Title.
GT2850.A6643 2011
394.1'2—dc22   2010033632

    Printed in China
       (hc) 10 9 8 7 6 5 4 3 2 1
       (sc) 10 9 8 7 6 5 4 3 2 1

Display type set in Grilled Cheese and
    text type set in Stone Sans
Color separations by Chroma Graphics,
    Singapore
Printed and bound February 2011 in Nansha,
    Guangdong, China, by Everbest Printing
    Company, Ltd. through Four Colour
    Imports Ltd., Louisville, Kentucky
Production supervision by Brian G. Walker
Designed by Susan Mallory Sherman

Introduction

Every day when she was ready to put dinner on the table, my mom would yell out the window: Georgie-e-e-e, *ven a COMER!* which translates from Spanish into English as: Georgie-e-e-e, come and EAT!

My dad was home from work, and my sister and I had to wash up and sit down to eat. That was when we could share our stories of the day.

The one thing that all people in the world have in common is that they eat to live. But eating is also an opportunity for us to come together to share food and friendship. When, how, what, where, and why we eat are as varied as the many peoples of the world.

While I was still in elementary school, the world opened up to me when I visited my classmates' homes, where I tasted so many foods from faraway places. My friends also liked to come to my house after school because my mother always gave us Mexican hot chocolate with tacos.

So now I'd like to invite you to

Come and Eat!

When we are born the first thing we do is cry. Why? Because we're hungry.

So our mother holds and nurses us—that's our first meal.

Over time we learn to eat solid foods.

It's a big day when we can feed ourselves.

While we sleep, we "fast," which means we don't eat. When we wake up, we "break" our fast by eating breakfast.

Around noontime we stop what we're doing to have lunch.

Schoolchildren eat in the cafeteria.

Workers eat on the job site.

At the end of the day, we have dinner, or supper, the main meal of the day. Some people say a prayer, or grace, to give thanks for the food on their table.

When we share a meal, we can also share our thoughts and feelings. Older people who live alone welcome a friend who brings them dinner and stays to visit.

At the table we learn the ways of our family and our culture.

Many people eat with knives, forks, and spoons using table manners that vary from country to country.

In some Asian countries people use chopsticks to eat.

Many foods are easier to eat with your fingers.

In some countries people eat only with their fingers. In India people use two fingers to scoop up food and then slide the food into their mouths with their thumb.

In Tibet people drink soup directly from the bowl.

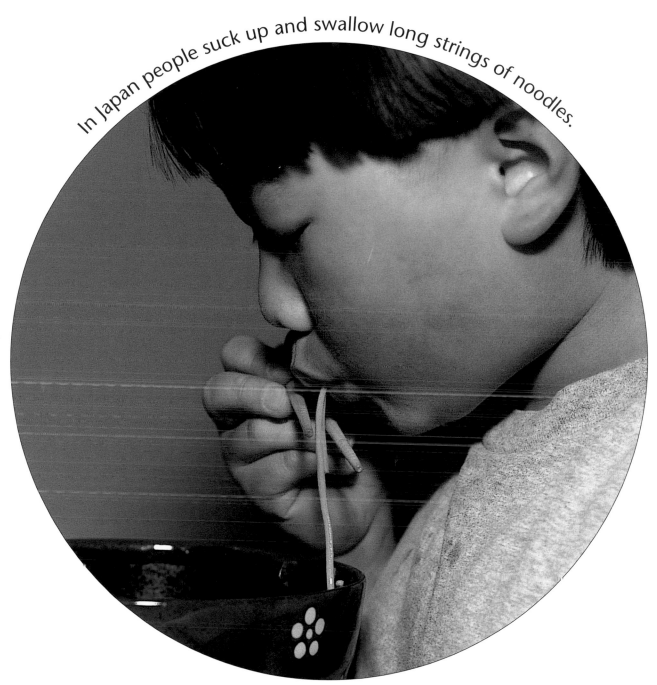

In Japan people suck up and swallow long strings of noodles.

It's amazing how quickly a meal can be finished!

Fufu is a favorite Nigerian delicacy. It's a cassava root that is ground up like mashed potatoes.

Guests sit on mats as the host passes around a bowl of water for them to wash their hands. Each diner then scoops up some *fufu* and rolls it into a small ball. This is then used to pick up meat, vegetables, and sauces from serving bowls.

After a prayer Tibetans eat delicious meat dumplings called *momos*. Tibetans use their fingers to dip each *momo* into a spicy sauce before eating it.

The tortilla is the ancient bread of the Mexicans. There are many ways to eat with it. You can roll meat and vegetables into a tortilla to make a taco or burrito.

Or a tortilla can serve as a plate, a spoon, and even a napkin. A stack of tortillas holds meat and vegetables. Pieces torn from the bottom are used to scoop up food from the top.

Wipe your mouth with the last piece of tortilla, then gobble it up.

When a Chinese family gathers to eat, everyone helps themselves to the food in the middle of the table and adds it to their bowls of rice.

Muslim friends remove their shoes to kneel on beautiful rugs to pray before sharing a meal.

Then platters of food are served. Men and boys usually eat together on one rug, while women and girls dine on another. The meal gives each group a chance to celebrate their brotherhood and sisterhood.

Warm weather is an invitation for families to pack a picnic basket and head outside. A donkey comes in handy to carry the food. The day is spent playing games, telling stories, wading in a stream, and, of course, eating food.

Cooking around a campfire is fun for the whole family.

Eating is also a way to celebrate a special event.

It's fun to dress up for special occasions.

People from Polynesian islands celebrate with a luau, or feast. While a pig is roasted over a fire, men make another fire in a pit and fill it with stones. Then they cover fish and vegetables wrapped in banana leaves with foil before putting them on the hot stones and burying them to cook.

Polynesians cool off by drinking coconut water. When dinner's ready, they feast at a table covered in banana leaves.

Different cultures celebrate holidays with special foods.

On Hanukkah, the Jewish festival of lights, delicious potato pancakes are served.

In Sweden, Saint Lucia's Day marks the start of Christmas celebrations. In the dark of early morning, the oldest daughter in a family puts on a white gown, a red sash, and a wreath with lighted candles. She brightens the dark winter morning by singing as she brings coffee with saffron-flavored buns to wake up her father.

Hispanic people prepare for Christmas with Las Posadas. Children dressed as Mary, Joseph, and the shepherds sing in front of eight houses, asking for shelter. Singers inside each house send them away. But at the ninth house, the pilgrims are invited in to share hot chocolate and *bizcochitos*, the traditional holiday cookies made with anise and cinnamon.

But people don't need a special event or holiday to come together to share a meal. The act of "breaking bread" together invites friendship, laughter, and good feelings. We may sit down next to a stranger, but by the end of the meal, we have become friends. Eating together becomes a ceremony to celebrate life.

Acknowledgments

My thanks go to the many people who allowed me to photograph them and then invited me to share their meal. Jamilah Abdullah, Gasali O. Adeyemo, Helga Ancona for the page 27 photo, Brittany Apodaca, Stuart Ashman family, Lapka and Tashi Dolma, Sharon Fernandez, Diyanira Anez Salas, Vanessa Garcia, Fabian Garcia, Heather Harr and family, Carolyne Hummer, Laura Husar, Beanie Kaman and Zane Wood, Tony McCarty of The Kitchen Angels, Mira Keene, Kent Kirkpatrick and family, Shizuko and Yasushi Kobayashi, Tamara Lichtenstein and Sienna Bergt, Alfonso Chavez Lujan, Nancy and Ted Meredith, the MacMillan family, Pete Martinez and family, Rafiu Aderemi Mustapha, Tevita Naulu and family, Catherine Oppenheimer, Michael Patterson and family, George Rivera and Kyu-hee Lee, Susan Griggs and family, Raquel Rivera, Manuel Sanchez and family, David Scheinbaum and Janet Russek, Talia St. Clair, Lisa M. Thomas-Adeyemo, Abayomi M. Tiamiyu, Tashi Tsering, Tenjin, Tsechokillsen, Katherine and Joel Van Essen, Rabia Van Hatum, Helena and Harald von Sydow, Claudia Vorch and the folks at The Commons, Ewan Young and family, Lucia Lopez, Keenan McDonald, and Hannah Manoff.

Author's Note

As a photographer and filmmaker I've had the good
fortune to travel to many places around the world. After a
day's work, the friendships I made were celebrated by sitting down
and sharing a meal together. In Hong Kong I was invited by the Chinese
film crew to celebrate the end of the job with a Korean meal. In Pakistan a
farm owner invited us to join him in a meal that was served only by men. We sat
cross-legged on beautiful carpets, and I tasted many foods for the first time.

I learned a different way to eat tortillas when I first traveled alone to Mexico after graduating
from high school. I arrived in a small town during market day. The crowds made way for four men
who were shouting and carrying a flat wooden tub filled with barbecued meat. They set the tub on
sawhorses and began to sell the meat by weight. The savory smell of the meat made me hungry.

So first I went to a lady selling tortillas and bought a stack. Then I returned to the meat vendor
and bought a half kilo to put on my tortillas. Next I went to another lady to buy vegetables,
which went on top of the meat. Balancing this pile of food, I sat on the street curb
alongside the *cargadores*, the porters who hauled goods to the market. As the
heavily loaded donkeys went by, I ate and talked with the men sitting next
to me—it was more fun than eating from dishes! Between bites we
got to know each other and became friends. They showed me
places and people to photograph—I would never have
found these by myself. And that's how I do
my books today.